P9-CJI-839

The Impatient Patient's Hospital Survival Guide

# AND HOW ARE WE feeling Today!?

*The Impatient Patient's Hospital Survival Guide*

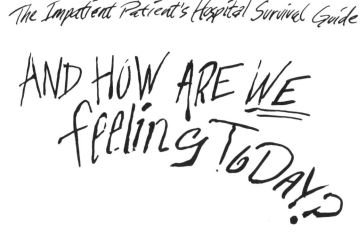
AND HOW ARE WE feeling TODAY?!?

KATHRYN HAMMER

CONTEMPORARY BOOKS

**Library of Congress Cataloging-in-Publication Data**

Hammer, Kathryn L.
    And how are we feeling today? : The impatient patient's
hospital survival guide / Kathryn L. Hammer.
        p.   cm.
    ISBN 0-8092-3834-9 (paper)
    1. Hospitals—Humor.   I. Title.
PN6231.H63H36    1993
362.1'1027—dc20                                    92-38382
                                                        CIP

Cover design by Mark Anderson
Interior illustrations by Mark Anderson

Published by Contemporary Books
A division of NTC/Contemporary Publishing Group, Inc.
4255 West Touhy Avenue, Lincolnwood (Chicago), Illinois 60712-1975 U.S.A.
Copyright © 1993 by NTC/Contemporary Publishing Group, Inc.
All rights reserved. No part of this book may be reproduced, stored in a
retrieval system, or transmitted in any form or by any means, electronic,
mechanical, photocopying, recording, or otherwise, without the prior written
permission of NTC/Contemporary Publishing Group, Inc.
Printed in the United States of America
International Standard Book Number: 0-8092-3834-9

99  00  01  02  03  04  VP  23  22  21  20  19  18  17  16  15  14  13  12  11  10  9  8

To Jon, my husband, my best friend, the love of my life,
whose bedside manner could cure anybody

# CONTENTS

Acknowledgments.........................ix

Introduction

*Why you need this book*....................1

1 Preparing for the Hospital Experience
*A docile patient is a happy patient*............5

2 Hospital Policies
*Rules made up while under the influence
of nitrous oxide*.........................17

3 Your Medical Team
*Getting to know your captors*................27

4 Hospital Food
*An oxymoron*..............................49

5 Procedures and Diagnostic Tests
*Your life as a laboratory mouse*..............55

6 Surgery
*The cutting edge of health care*..............77

7 Speaking the Language
*Bilingualism: a chronic condition*............91

8  Hospital Fashion
   *Feeling like hell is no excuse for looking
   like it* . . . . . . . . . . . . . . . . . . . . . . . . . . . . . .99

9  Dollars and Cents
   *For little more than it would cost to outfit
   Communist China in Pendleton blazers,
   you too can have surgery.* . . . . . . . . . . . . . .107

   Appendix
   *An apparently functionless part that should
   be removed* . . . . . . . . . . . . . . . . . . . . . . . . . . .115

# ACKNOWLEDGMENTS

To the Good Guys at Community North Hospital in Indianapolis (you know who you are)—for compassion, care, morphine, and sherbet and for resisting the impulse to pull the plug when you had the chance.

To doctors who paid attention in med school on the days it counted.

To my twin sister, Anita—for practicing medicine without a license, using love, laughter, and purple eyeshadow; and for all your help and encouragement in everything.

To Mom and Dad—for your love and support in countless ways.

To all of my family—Nick, Chris, Terry, Molly, in-laws—for being there when I need you.

To my dear friends—for keeping me humble and laughing and loved . . . especially Potter, who keeps me weird.

To my editor, Linda Gray—for sharing my sense of the absurd and an affinity for whipped cream.

To my agent, Nancy Yost, and electronic advisor, Harry Arnston—for solid business advice.

And, finally, to the dedicated professionals of the entire health-care industry—for making America a great place to get sick.

# INTRODUCTION

## WHY YOU NEED THIS BOOK

*HOSPITAL—from the Latin*
hospes, *meaning* guest

*Saddam Hussein referred to
his hostages as "guests"...*

Recent studies have shown that the average American is far more likely to stay in a hospital than a bed and breakfast in Bora Bora. This is because Americans become sick or injured more often than they inherit vast sums of money. Yet there are roughly 17 billion guidebooks on places you will never visit as long as you live. You own guidebooks to shopping, wining and dining, fishing, elk hunting, Amish butter making, casinos, cemeteries, and the Great Flea Markets of the Kalahari. You have learned the skill of bartering your spouse for strong oxen and a clean bed.

Your hospital savvy, however, could fit into a specimen cup. It's time to *wake up and smell the barium.*

This handy, informative manual explains everything you need to know about hospitals—in words that actual people use instead of words that doctors use. You'll learn what they really do in there . . . things involving garden implements and toxic waste.

Reading this guidebook will give you all the resolve you need to decide never to be sick or injured again, so help you God.

(Author's note: For reasons of convenience, not sexism, this book uses masculine pronouns for doctors and feminine pronouns for nurses. The use of "he/she," "him or her," "himself or herself," destroys the flow, and I don't want to hear about it from any of you. Write your own awkwardly phrased, politically correct book.)

# 1
# PREPARING FOR THE HOSPITAL EXPERIENCE

## A DOCILE PATIENT IS A HAPPY PATIENT

*Please deposit all valuables,
personal belongings, and
modesty with the admissions
officer. They will be returned
to you at the end of your stay.*

## THE PROPER PATIENT

The Proper Patient is meek and submissive. You, however, are probably assertive and pigheaded.

If you apologize when someone hits you with his car ("Oh, I'm so sorry! I should've known not to walk on a sidewalk so close to the street"), you're a hospital staff's dream.

If, however, you're the type who writes letters to the editor, returns defective merchandise, and flips off Hell's Angels for a lark, you may have a teensy bit of adjusting to do.

Because the key to a rewarding, successful hospital experience is the ability to remain passive and compliant while unspeakable indignities called "procedures" are performed upon you for no apparent reason in well-trafficked public hallways by people wearing shower caps from the Holiday Inn.

You are not allowed to comment on this. If you do, they will look at you as if you were wearing your underwear on your head.

### A WORD ABOUT PRIVACY

Expect as much privacy as a whale giving birth at Sea World.

Should you have an aversion to busloads of tour groups peering into your body cavities, *get over it*. At first you might find this difficult, but soon you'll be cooperating cheerfully with all affronts to your dignity and inviting the flower delivery boy to have a look-see.

There is, of course, a "privacy" curtain you can pull around your bed, the *actual* function of which is to induce cardiac arrest when someone creeps up and whips it open. When closed, it serves as a signal to the general public that something *highly personal* is being done to you, at which time you will be visited by: nurses, doctors, volunteers, physical therapists, chaplains, occupational therapists, other patients, technicians, orderlies, interns, housekeepers, observers, patient reps, dietitians, accounting personnel, the mobile gift shop, family, friends, neighbors, insurance adjusters, social workers, clinicians, consultants, maintenance engineers, Brownie troops, roaming hordes of assorted do-gooders, eleven lords a-leaping, and a partridge in a pear tree.

## BUT HOW DO I PREPARE FOR THIS?

You say it would be helpful to practice being a Proper Patient ahead of time? Of course it would!

An excellent method is to become a hostage in an unfriendly nation. Unfortunately, this is not always convenient. Fortunately, the preadmission exercises on the next page can help you become compliant, passive, and less embarrassed by things that *ought* to embarrass you.

. . . . . . . . . . . . . . . . . . . . . . . . . . . . . . . . . . . .

## SOME HANDY EXERCISES YOU CAN DO RIGHT IN YOUR OWN HOME TO PREPARE FOR THE HOSPITAL EXPERIENCE

- Lay nude on the front lawn and ask the Chemlawn man to probe you with his applicator.
- Drink a quart of Sherwin-Williams Eggshell Beige One-Coat Coverage Interior Flat White #2. Then have your child stuff his Slinky down your throat.
- Put a real estate agent's "Open House" sign in your front yard and lie on your bed dressed in a paper napkin with straws stuck up your nose.
- Put your hand down the garbage disposal while practicing your smile and repeating, "Mild discomfort."
- Set your alarm to go off every ten minutes from 10:00 P.M. to 7:00 A.M., at which times you will alternately puncture your wrist with a Phillips screwdriver and stab yourself with a knitting needle.
- Remove all actual food from the house.
- With several strands of Christmas lights strung from a coat tree and onto yourself, walk *slowly* up and down the hall.
- Urinate into an empty lipstick tube.

. . . . . . . . . . . . . . . . . . . . . . . . . . . . . . . . . . . .

## PARTICIPATING IN YOUR OWN CARE WHILE REMAINING SILENT

Hospitals encourage patients to be involved with their care and to ask questions. If, however, you actually do that, the medical staff will become disoriented and flustered. Their pulse rates will become erratic, and they will look at you as if you were a muskmelon suddenly possessed of the power of speech.

They will notify Administration. Stat. Someone will be sent to "handle" you, such as a chaplain or a psychiatrist.

A Patient Representative will pay a visit to determine if you fit the profile of Someone Likely to Spill His Guts on "Geraldo." She'll say things like "I can appreciate that" and "I understand your concern." Of course these are lies, because she is all of eighteen and her major health concern is split ends.

If you're a Good Patient—docile, passive, and oh, so grateful—they will be nice to you. They'll believe you when you say it hurts, and they'll give you orange sherbet. They'll close your door and call you "sweetie."

If, on the other hand, you're labeled a Bad Patient (as a result of Bad Behavior, such as screaming, "You ignorant cow!" when they miss a vein), they'll make faces behind your back and roll their eyes a lot. They'll hide your glasses and put the water *just* out of reach. They'll disconnect your number on the call-button panel, prop open your door, and schedule your room for drywall repair.

## SELECTING THE RIGHT HOSPITAL

If you've just been in a DC-10 midair collision, you won't have much say over where you're taken. If, however, you have the luxury of time, consider the following when choosing a hospital:

### WHAT'S IN A NAME?

- St. Francis Hospital. Francis is the patron saint of animals. Unless you are going to be spayed or wormed, select again.
- St. Anthony's Hospital. Anthony is the patron saint of missing things. What is it they are missing? Sponges? Surgical instruments? Internal organs?
- University Hospital and Research Center. Expect to be the Show and Tell project for busloads of foreign exchange students.
- St. Catherine's. Catherine of Alexandria was tortured to death on a wheel, whereby her limbs were torn from her without anesthesia.

## WHAT THE HOSPITALS REALLY MEAN BY "PARTICIPATING IN YOUR CARE"

1. Agree to everything

2. Assume the required diagnostic positions

3. Sign the release forms

4. Cough/spit/swallow/breathe/urinate on command

5. Pay your bill

## WHAT THEY DON'T MEAN

1. Ask questions

2. Suggest anything

3. Complain

Avoid these hospitals altogether:

- Claus Von Bulow Memorial
- Our Lady of Adhesions
- Sacred Heart Failure
- Billy Bob's Surgical Center and Bait Shop
- Gallbladders R Us

## TRACK RECORD

Take into consideration the reputation of the hospital. Ask the following questions:

- Has this hospital ever been featured on "60 Minutes"?
- Does this hospital run display ads in the classifieds offering free legal counsel to anyone who will work there?
- Is their poison-control hotline connected to the kitchen?
- Do they advertise with a 900 number on matchbooks?

Also, be wary of the following:

- A large number of hearses in the parking lot
- Dumpsters overflowing with beer cans
- Cobwebs on the employees' soap dispenser
- The use of Shell No-Pest Strips as mobiles over the nursery cribs

## ADMISSION:
## CHECKING IN TO HOTEL HELL

Preparing yourself for hospital admission is easy. Simply travel to Moscow and attempt to buy a coat or a can of tuna. This process accurately simulates the waiting process of check-in. You will be given a number, in case you're there to buy bagels. There will be reading material available to pass the time:

- *Addiction: Breaking the Cycle Through Our Highly Profitable Crisis Center That Just Happens to Be Affiliated with This Hospital*
- *Breast Self-Examination for Fun and Profit*
- *Multilevel Marketing of Unnecessary Diagnostic Tests*

Once you've finished those highly entertaining, uplifting brochures, you can read the NO SMOKING sign. Then you can direct your attention to the following magazines of interest to the average adult:

- *Highlights for Children* (January 1967 issue)
- *Composting Quarterly* (with cover torn off)
- *Guide to Beauty School Scholarships* (with 10 percent tuition discount coupon removed)

Eventually, if they feel like it, they'll call your number. The clerk will then excuse herself for thirty minutes. When she returns, you'll be asked the following questions:

Name

Address

Date of birth

Age (they can't figure this out from your date of birth)

Height (to size you for a gown that falls short of your buttocks)

Weight (for scheduling appropriately hefty orderlies to move you)

Occupation (to screen out contingency lawyers)

Religion (just in case)

Next of kin (who do they stick with the bill if you croak?)

Education (to see how much they can put past you)

Salary (helpful in determining number of tests ordered)

Insurance (to determine length of stay)

Family's health history (marketing info for patient prospecting)

You'll need to produce your insurance card, as it is Standard Procedure to assume you're a financially insolvent, pathological liar. You must also sign a statement designating as collateral your house, car, stamp collection, and any marketable internal organs.

Eventually they'll get to the part about why you're there. They require lengthy details of your symptoms, a complete report on which is sitting there in triplicate. They do this to test the consistency of your story. You'll repeat this nine times to people who are paid to catch you in a lie and find more expensive stuff wrong with you.

You'll then wait two hours while they find a bed. Apparently, beds are difficult to locate and are frequently misplaced. This also affords them time to run a Dun & Bradstreet on you as well as a computer check to see if you've ever filed a malpractice suit. Emergency admission is similar but lengthier, due to your unconscious state.

Once your condition has deteriorated sufficiently, you'll be taken to your room.

# 2
# HOSPITAL POLICIES

## RULES MADE UP WHILE UNDER THE INFLUENCE OF NITROUS OXIDE

*In the alleged interest of its patients, the Administration enforces certain policies, which may or may not be rational, for the convenience of the staff. The Policy Board shall be composed of retired Department of Motor Vehicles clerks, State Fair parking attendants, and suspended IRS auditors.*

## A PARTIAL LISTING OF HOSPITAL POLICIES YOU NEED TO KNOW

*Patients must not be allowed to be alone and uninterrupted for more than 10 minutes at a time.*
*Exceptions to this rule:*

1. When patient is ringing the call button

2. When patient's monitor is beeping and the nurse is on break

3. When the only programs on TV are "Victory Garden," "American Gladiators," "Green Acres," and highlights of the monster truck competition

*Sleep is discouraged, except when induced by medical personnel for their own convenience.*

Many procedures require the patient to be alert in order to fully appreciate the embarrassing nature and extreme discomfort of the processes involved.

Sleep is also disruptive to the schedules of nurses and technicians who have a whole list of things they must Do To You before they can go home, such as monitoring you for sleep disorders.

However, sleep may be chemically induced if:

1. You are starting to feel better and want to go home

2. The doctor is getting ready to pay his Daily Visit

3. You're watching a "Geraldo" segment called "Hospital Horrors"

*All procedures must make the patient feel like an ass.*

One of the easiest ways to accomplish this is to have you assume embarrassing positions in various stages of undress. This is a medical variation on the game "Twister". "OK. What I want you to do now is lean over this board until your nose touches that dot. OK. Now stick your butt up as high as you can. OK. Now raise your right leg like a crane. Good. Now do an impression of Eleanor Roosevelt singing 'I Feel Pretty.' "

*Anything that feels good is medically unsound.*

Nothing comfortable will be permitted when something uncomfortable will do. For this reason, you will be given intramuscular shots with caustic liquids instead of using the medication in one of the 42 intravenous tubes already stuck in your veins.

And since plain vanilla X-rays are not particularly uncomfortable, the temperature in the room will be lowered until you are the proper shade of blue. You'll then be made to lie in a position you might assume after a fall from an Alpine ski lift.

*All hospital food must be inspected and approved by the American Kennel Club.*

Despite these high standards, hospital cooks are instructed not to expend time and effort on attractive, tasty food preparation. The patient is, after all, sick. Sick people throw up. Meals are prepared from items regularly consumed by cultures featured in Time-Life Books' *Strange but True* series. These items can be supplemented with various nondairy polymers as well as copious amounts of artificial colors called *gelatin.*

None of this will be of a color that actually occurs in nature.

*Meals must be delivered at the following times:*

- When you are in X-ray, physical therapy, or surgery
- When you are undergoing a procedure involving nerve endings
- When you are heavily sedated and drooling on the pillow
- When you are on the bedpan
- When you are upchucking the previous meal

*A separate blood sample must be drawn for each separate test by separate technicians, spacing themselves 20 minutes apart, from 5:00 A.M. to 11:00 P.M.*

Hospitals view blood as a renewable resource, like zucchini. Even though only a tiny amount of blood is needed for each test, you can always make more, which is much more convenient than having to divvy up one sample. Technicians, many of whom are former post-hole diggers, spend hundreds of hours learning how to draw blood by practicing on oranges. Consequently, should there ever be an outbreak of serious illness in the produce department of the supermarket, they are ready to spring into action. This, however, has no bearing on you, since oranges don't have nerve endings.

*The patient's door must be left open.*

The door to your room is there only as a handy place to post signs, such as public announcements of your urine output.

It cannot be closed to afford privacy or quiet. Nurses must be able to dash in quickly to catch you violating one of their policies, like sleeping.

*Nurses may not cut patients' toenails.*

There is no known reason for this policy.

It is interesting to note that while nurses routinely insert foot-long metal needles into your veins and shave your private areas with straight razors such as you might find in teenage slasher movies, they are not allowed to cut your toenails.

If your hospital stay is lengthy, you may wish to consider calling in a dog groomer. Or perhaps retain the toenails for use as a handy letter opener for all those get-well cards.

*The results of all diagnostic tests must indicate the need for other diagnostic tests, until the patient gets fed up or the insurance runs out, whichever comes first.*

In an effort to maximize the revenue potential of each patient, as many tests as possible will be performed.

Additional tests may then be ordered to test for side effects of previous tests. Repeats of the original tests will then be performed to confirm the initial results, and further studies will be made to evaluate the effect of the repeat tests on side effects caused by additional tests. Got it?

*Hospital policy prohibits backseat driving and armchair quarterbacking by family members.*

Hospitals treat family members with the same warmth they would extend to large rodents. They become highly agitated if relatives make ignorant, untrained observations, such as:

- "Wouldn't Mother be just a wee bit more comfortable if the IV tube were disentangled from around her neck?"

- "Is it normal to have all that blood spurting from Grandpa's catheter?"
- "Why is the heart monitor sounding the Civil Defense Alert signal?"

Hospital personnel deal with such nonsense firmly and swiftly. They will explain, in tones reserved for naughty servants, that everything is under control and that they are Professionals, whereas you are simply "well-meaning," a euphemism for "pain in the ass."

In addition to being annoying, armchair quarterbacking can distract highly trained medical personnel from Important Hospital Routines, such as rattling venetian blinds at odd intervals.

*Humor is inappropriate in the hospital setting.*

Joking around with the doctors and nurses is risky business and will not be tolerated, because many of your seriously intelligent medical types have the sense of humor of Vaseline.

This is due to an accident at birth, wherein their humor was sucked out through their ears with a Shop-Vac. Any residue is surgically removed in the last year of residency.

Trying to engage them in witty repartee is like trying to explain electricity to your cat:

DR.: "Have you had a bowel movement today?"

You: "Why, yes. I gave birth to a nine-pound porcupine just moments ago."

Dr. (suspiciously): "I thought you said your tubes were tied."

He will then make extensive notes on your chart and schedule you for genetic testing.

Humor is, of course, in the eye of the beholder, and it is foolish to entrust it to people who have freely chosen as their life's work installing periscopes in other people's rectums.

*Patients must walk except when able. This does not include use of the bathroom.*

Immediately following surgery, you will be required to take a walking tour of the hospital while dragging your IV pole and 14 miles of tubing. You will not, however, be allowed to walk eight feet to the bathroom but instead will be forced to use a bedpan.

It is evidently easier to mount a hard metal object backward, sprawl over it, and overcome several decades of toilet training that have conditioned you against voiding while prone, and then have a team of housekeepers change your bedding as you balance yourself precariously on the railings.

The bathroom, it must be remembered, is there solely for the janitorial personnel, who are required to flush your toilet continuously between the hours of 2:00 A.M. and 3:00 A.M. for reasons too technical and medical for laypeople like you to understand.

*Patients should be assigned to the most incompatible roommate possible in their semiprivate room.*

If you are extremely ill, you will be bunking with someone who's merely resting after an exhausting whirlwind weekend with lottery officials after his record $98.5 million win. He will have an extended family the size of the population of Guadalajara.

If you are a deliriously happy new mother, you will have a roommate who's undergoing a court-ordered lobotomy to control her homicidal episodes.

# 3
# YOUR MEDICAL TEAM
## GETTING TO KNOW YOUR CAPTORS

*Many successful nurses and doctors got their starts by pulling the wings off butterflies and tumble-drying the neighbor's cat.*

Your Medical Team consists of people who are not like you and me. They are Different.

- As children, they exhibited an unusual aptitude for medical procedure. For example, they were adept at forcing the star shape into the round hole in the Shape Sorter. And pounding wooden pegs from the toy workbench into the doll's anatomically correct areas. And placing Barbie into My Merry Kitchen Oven at 350° for two hours, after which she gets a lube job in the Fisher-Price Garage.
- They fantasize about Edward Scissorhands.
- Their hobbies and pastimes include cleaning catfish and cruising the state fair poultry barn with a meat thermometer.
- Their idea of a good joke is hiding bits of tin foil in a sandwich and giving it to a friend who's just had dental work.

## DOCTORS

First, you must come to grips with the fact that Marcus Welby does not exist.

It's true. He was cancelled some years ago after well-organized lobbying efforts by the American Medical Association, who feared that the public might actually believe in kindly family doctors who call you up at home and say, "Hi. Just calling to see how you're feeling today. Is there anything at all Consuelo or I could do for you, like shovel your walk or bring you a freshly baked pie made with peaches we grew ourselves?"

## SELECTING A DOCTOR

It's best to have a doctor picked out in a̱
Otherwise, one will be assigned to you by ̱ ̱ple
who think orange plaid flannel is a fine tuxedo
fabric.
  Selecting a doctor used to be easy. In 1700
B.C., the laws of Hammurabi stated that a physician causing injury to a patient would have his
hand cut off. Patients in search of a doctor back
then only needed to be observant—and to avoid
doctors with names like "Lefty."
  Today's patients must be more sophisticated.
They must observe the following criteria when
selecting a doctor:

. . . . . . . . . . . . . . . . . . . . . . . . . . . . . . . . . . . .

### AVOID DOCTORS WHOSE
### WAITING ROOMS

- Are decorated with paintings of dogs play-
  ing poker
- Have the newspaper obituaries highlighted
  in yellow
- Are decorated with apothecary jars containing former patients
- Frequently have chalk body outlines on the
  carpet
- Have pornographic magazines with the
  anatomic parts labeled
- Have a life-sized, bronze statue of themselves, with flowers, votive candles, and a
  kneeling bench at its foot

. . . . . . . . . . . . . . . . . . . . . . . . . . . . . . . . . . . .

. . . . . . . . . . . . . . . . . . . . . . . . . . . . . . . . .

## AVOID DOCTORS WHOSE

- Favorite movies are *Silence of the Lambs* and *Amityville Horror*
- Diplomas are printed in green crayon
- Lab coats appear to be freshly tie-dyed with Rit Raspberry
- Muzak is tuned to Ozzy Osbourne
- Favorite sport is baby-seal hunting

. . . . . . . . . . . . . . . . . . . . . . . . . . . . . . . . .

Once you've decided on a doctor, other doctors whom you've never met will be called in to consult. They are usually specialists who are available at a moment's notice because they have no patients of their own, for reasons listed in the above criteria.

## FACTS ABOUT DOCTORS

*Doctors enter the medical field because it's the only profession other than cocaine dealer where they can make a kajillion dollars and wear a beeper.*

Persons who are dull and unattractive find that being a doctor is a helpful dating aid. "Physician" is one of the few titles that can guarantee a good table at the snottiest restaurants.

It's also one of the few career options available to people whose talent in the high school variety show was artificially inseminating dairy cattle.

*If egos were throat glands, most doctors would
be dragging around enormous goiters.*

They believe they are genetically superior to
philistines such as you who merely sell widgets
and bowl on Thursdays, whereas *they* Save Lives
and Enhance Quality of Life on a daily basis.
They are acutely aware that they get news of
medical facts and startling breakthroughs from
*The New England Journal of Medicine,* whereas
you get them from Regis Philbin.

Consequently, you will be dealt with in tones
reserved for putting senile people back to bed
after they've wandered off into the broom closet.

*Doctors do not think you are one bit funny.*

Your pathetic attempts to lighten your stress
with humor are just one more reason why they
want to slice you open with a knife.

Usually, they don't even *know* when you're
joking. Your doctor will nod somberly when you
express concern that your condition is caused by a
diet lacking in Cool Whip. Occasionally, in the
interest of Effective Patient Rapport, he will force
a patronizing grunt, making him appear consti-
pated.

*Doctors merely "practice" medicine.*

The term "medical practice" originated when
two doctors from New York discovered that their
golf games improved remarkably after each
round. This led them to the startling conclusion

that if practice lowers their golf scores, why, maybe practice might lower the incidence of error on the operating table!

This concept caught on, and millions of doctors now practice their art every day on people like you, in preparation for the day they treat someone important, like their tax accountant.

*Doctors didn't know all that technical medical stuff until they learned it, and if you learned it, you'd know it too.*

Doctors do not want you to realize this, as it may cause you to actually understand what they're saying, which, of course, is:

"We can't be sure, but all indications suggest that your manifold is experiencing a subacute proxosis with your gyroscopic ventricular xylophone. Your homophones are way up, and your nympho counts are borderline low, so we'll be watching your milivanilis. I suggest you take it easy for a while."

*Doctors have absolutely no clue what's wrong with you* until you tell them!

They'll ask you what seems to be the trouble, where does it hurt, when did it start, does this make it worse, etc. Then they'll proceed to tell it back to you in their own words and your mouth will fall open in amazement at their uncanny accuracy.

It is important that you make them think it

was all their idea, since you are obviously a victim of cross-species breeding.

*The doctor will respond to anything you have to say about your condition or treatment in the same manner as the Pope listening to yet another young peasant girl describe how the Blessed Mother appeared to her in a bag of Chee·tos.*

Let's say you were to point out a glaring cause-and-effect situation: projectile vomiting and large, pus-filled boils occur immediately following your medication. You meekly suggest that perhaps, just maybe, you oughtn't take any more of that stuff.

Your doctor will smile knowingly and write condescending little notes in your file: "Patient unwilling to retain full prescribed dosage. Probable hysteria. Increase dosage."

*Doctors become disoriented and confused if you try to talk to them.*

Although he may come in for his Daily Visit and ask how you're doing, do not be misled into thinking that a dialogue should ensue.

This is not a cocktail party. The doctor is allowed to charge you vast sums of money just for having set foot in the room. He doesn't do dialogue. If you want to talk to someone, he will call the chaplain.

*The doctor's associate will be a non-English-speaking person from an Emerging Nation, in native ceremonial garb.*

This associate is allowed to substitute for the doctor in order to collect the Daily Fee. He will not actually say anything to you, but will lift up your gown and solemnly peer, poke, and prod about places totally unrelated to your condition.

*As patients, doctors are the biggest babies.*

Any nurse will tell you she'd rather care for a diseased yeti than tend to a hospitalized doctor.

Doctors are obnoxious patients because they know what euphemisms such as "momentary discomfort" really mean. You can't trick them into submitting to the kinds of things they inflict on their own patients. They also demand real food and privacy—things hospitals aren't prepared to provide.

## NURSES

No one has more influence over the quality of your hospital stay, with the possible exception of the insurance company and that friend who sneaks in the chocolates.

### THINGS TO REMEMBER ABOUT NURSES

*They all entered the profession because they wanted to Help People.*

This is also what one wants to do if one wants to become Miss Alabama. However, lacking the talent to sing an aria while twirling a fiery baton, they entered the medical field.

*They're likely to be a tad off.*

What these nurses didn't realize until they had already spent $75,000 on their educations is that Helping People involves things like vomit and doing distasteful things to distasteful people's distasteful parts. So they're likely to be just *a tad off.*

*You must take care not to offend them.*

Deal gently with anyone who's *a tad off,* especially one who carries automotive tools, has access to your body cavities, and has the authority to make you do the lambada with a rubber hose.

For example, it may not be wise to suggest that your nurse reminds you of what would happen if Roseanne Arnold and Mr. Ed had a child. Whap! Catheter time! Likewise, criticizing her blood-letting technique is likely to garner you a set of collapsed veins, and a casual comment questioning her response time to the call button is begging for a sharply lowered dose of pain medication.

*Some nurses are better than others, which you'll discover quickly, since a new one will be assigned to you every 30 minutes.*

Apparently, good nurses burn out rapidly. They must be gathered up and shipped to sanitariums, at which point a new supply is whisked in.

Just when you think, "Aha! A warm, wonderful, compassionate human being with cool hands and excellent medical skills who will protect me," they will whisk her off to the sanitarium. She will be replaced by someone with the manual dexterity of a tranquilized gibbon who thinks illness is a character weakness.

*Most of your diagnosis and treatment is in the nurse's hands.*

It's therefore important to remember that the nursing profession is not a variation on the flight-attendant profession. Although they'll occasionally offer pillows, inquire, "Jell-O, broth, or morphine?" and position oxygen masks comfortably over your nose and mouth, nurses are highly educated professionals.

The doctor has no clue as to what's going on with you except for what the nurse tells him, since he's only with you for 2½ minutes each day to collect the Daily Fee. So the nurse will guide him in the right direction, taking pains to make the doctor think it was all his idea.

*Nurses can be allies or adversaries.*

If the nurse is on your side, she can suggest holding off on some of those More Painful Unnecessary Tests. If she is not on your side, she will hint to the doctor that maybe your case is more complicated than he thought, and had he considered that agonizing test involving electricity?

*Nurses will address you using terms of endearment.*

In an effort to make you feel more Comfortable and Cared For, nurses will call you by nicknames normally reserved for close personal relationships. This also eliminates the need to know your real name. You are no longer Mr., Mrs., Professor, Judge, or Reverend. You are now Honey, Sweetie, or Darlin'. (The *g* is always dropped in this term of endearment. Using the *g* means you are engaged.)

Nurses feel entitled to sound so chummy because of the extremely chummy things they will be doing to you.

*All nurses chew gum.*

They chew loudly and with a vengeance, and they are all very good at cracking and popping it—particularly the night nurses.

You'll learn to recognize them from their chewing cadence. Some nurses have a slow, deliberate rhythm that matches what they're doing, as if they have figured out how many chews and snaps equal an injection. With this technique, they can deliver accurate dosages in the dark.

Other nurses chew at high speed. These are the ones to watch out for, because they are very, very nervous.

*Nurses no longer wear white uniforms and starched caps.*

Recently, the nursing profession has come to realize that most serious industries do not require their employees to wear their children's origami projects on their heads.

There are 124 federally subsidized billion-dollar studies that demonstrate that the traditional white uniform and white nurse's cap create a barrier to effective Patient Interaction. Evidently, the patient comes to associate white uniforms and caps with pain, causing him to later flip out at weddings, lunging at the bride and screaming, "Don't come near me with that thing, you vile slut demon!"

*Nurses now wear shocking pink pants and tops.*

This is a really good disguise, because no patient would ever in a million years guess that someone dressed like a clerk at a discount store where they sell manufacturer's overstock glitter nail polish was actually a Trained Nurse.

Later, your subconscious figures out that pain and embarrassment should now be associated with *shocking pink pants and oversize tops.* This repressed hostility will resurface without warning the next time you see a rerun of "The Golden Girls."

*One of the most valuable functions your nurse will perform is intercepting illegible doctors' orders.*

The really good nurses have completed graduate studies in Reading Prescriptions Written in Non-Extant Languages by Physicians Apparently Suffering from Severe Neurological Disorders. This prevents much needless suffering on your part.

For example, she will intercede on your behalf when a team of surgeons is about to disfigure you by gently pointing out that the doctor's orders simply said, "Restrict spicy food," not "Remove spine and foot."

Similarly, she will notify pharmacy that, no, the doctor did not want you to have an STP Motor Oil enema—what he wrote was *"Stop monitoring in A.M."*

*Nurses will rate your pain on a scale from 1 to 10.*

They will ask you to assign a number to your degree of pain, with 1 being minimal and 10 the worst pain ever in the history of the universe. This is a trick.

If you say 10, they'll figure nothing they do to you could make it worse, so they can utilize procedures not normally perpetrated on live patients. Assigning a low number indicates a high pain threshold, which will make them think they can do more painful stuff to you without giving you painkillers.

Don't fall for this. Always give them a number like 7 or 8, while blinking back hot tears and forcing a pathetic smile.

## VOLUNTEERS

One of the more annoying species indigenous to the hospital is the Volunteer. Volunteers are abnormally chirpy, perky individuals whose only apparent job is filling your water pitcher.

They also want to Cheer You Up. They will proclaim you extraordinarily lucky because even though you are in intolerable pain, why, there are so many, many people worse off than you. ("There's a guy who had 22 operations without anesthesia, and just think, forty years ago people died from what you've got.")

There are four different kinds of Volunteers:

## SENIOR CITIZENS TRYING TO STAY ACTIVE

This group is composed of both men and women, often widowed, who find that their sick friends are too depressing. So they Stay Active by visiting sick strangers in the hospital.

These older volunteers will volunteer all sorts of personal information (which is why they call them volunteers) regarding *their* hospital stays and operations and the various career paths of their sons and daughters who *would* come home for a visit if only they weren't so terribly busy and successful.

The hospital is also a good place to meet Senior Citizens of the Opposite Sex Trying to Stay Active.

## INVOLVED TEENAGERS WITH A VISION

These are the ones who want to join the Peace Corps so they can teach Third World children the words to "Kumbaya." They want to buy the world a Coke. And they want to *Help You.*

(Besides, it looks good on a college application: *National Honor Society, Band, Earth Day Chairman, Hospital Volunteer.*)

They'll say things like "After every storm there's a rainbow" and "Today is the first day of the rest of your life." To which you will reply, "Suck an egg."

Other than that, they really don't have a clue what to say to you except to ask you how you're feeling, which should be evident from the fact that you're wired up like a Christmas tree.

## THE JUNIOR LEAGUER

She wears cunning little Lanz print dresses with dropped waists. She'll pluck the dead blossoms from your flower arrangements while filling you in on the progress of her herb garden.

Her ash-blond-starting-to-gray hair is in a chin-length bob or Dorothy Hamill wedge. She wears coral frost lipstick and has a great tan. Her children are all away at private colleges, and she has Some Time on Her Hands. "Do you play tennis?" she'll inquire. "No," you reply. "These IV lines keep tangling up in the net."

## OFFENDERS SENTENCED
## TO COMMUNITY SERVICE

These people are really thrilled to be here.

They find you distasteful and unpleasant. In fact, they find this whole idea an embarrassing bore.

They will shuffle into your room and just

stand there looking at your water pitcher. They hope you're in a coma.

You can have fun with these people. In a weak voice, cry out, "Water. Water." Beckon them with a trembling hand. Make them hold the cup to your parched lips while you sip through the bent plastic straw. Clutch their wrists desperately and wheeze, *"Help me . . . they're . . . trying . . . to kill . . . I know . . . too . . . much. . . ."*

With the exception of the Offenders, volunteers wouldn't know when to leave if the walls started to ooze slime, furniture began to fly about the room, and a pig's head with red glowing eyes roared, "GET . . . OUT . . . OF . . . HERE!!"

## CHAPLAIN

The hospital chaplain is there to scare the hell out of you. (Did someone place a frantic call for the last rites? Maybe the doctors aren't telling you everything. Father Mulcahey only showed up around the four-oh-seven-seventh when Hawkeye and Trapper John needed him to break the news about an amputation. . . . )

No one actually requests the chaplain; he just sort of appears. He's there for you, to talk and to share, if that's what you want, which of course you don't because you're sitting on the bedpan and you're only in here for a few tests anyway.

(Aren't you???)

The question must be asked: Why doesn't this person have his own parish? Can't he draw a congregation of his own? Why must he rely upon souls who are strapped down and sedated?

If you have not been exhibiting the Proper Patient Profile, the chaplain may be sent by Administration to "handle" you.

Using practiced, soothing tones perfected at wakes and funerals, he'll remind you that the meek shall inherit the earth and that God never gives us more than we can bear. *And, yes, my child, that includes enemas.*

He will attempt to Inspire You with a story of a permanently hospitalized young woman who, despite great pain and no limbs, knits mohair surgical gloves for the staff each Christmas.

*And . . .* (dramatic pause) . . . *she never complains.*

Have a nice day, my child.

## PHYSICAL AND OCCUPATIONAL THERAPISTS

Physical and occupational therapy are two distinct disciplines. You had better not confuse them, or they will *correct* you in the same tone Alex Trebek might use to chide a contestant for missing an obvious distinction: "An entomologist is, as we all know, one who studies *insects.* An etymologist, of course, studies *words.*"

No matter what is wrong with you, PTs and OTs assume that it has also affected your brain. So they will speak  v e r y  s l o w l y  and use simple words that You Can Understand. They all have taken speech training from Mr. Rogers.

If you address them by their correct, scientific titles, Physical and Occupational Terrorists, they will send you to Speech Therapy.

## PHYSICAL TERRORISTS

Regardless of the condition that brought you to the hospital, you will be taken to Physical Therapy.

Jagged bone protruding from your spine? Physical Therapy.

Brain tumor? Physical Therapy. Massive hemorrhage? Fever? Ringworm? Shock? Yup— Physical Therapy.

There, along with several other pajama-clad, drugged, pain-riddled patients with matted, unwashed hair, you will be put into a harness and made to walk with a therapist who has spent six years and $150,000 on schooling to learn how to keep from yelling, "WOULD YOU HURRY UP!"

Physical Terrorists will show you Exercises You Can Do, like moving your foot up and down, which you probably would never have thought of. This is why this 20-minute outing will cost you $543.

They will give you rubber bands to stretch and rubber balls to squeeze. Upon successful completion of a stretch or squeeze, they will react as though you had discovered cold fusion. They're easily impressed.

They will also put heat packs or ice packs on the Affected Part, whichever feels worse.

None of this, of course, can be done in your

own hospital room, for complicated medical reasons too complicated and medical to understand. The ordeal of being hoisted from bed to gurney, bounced about miles of public corridors, removed from gurney onto PT table, and then repeating the process all over again on the way back is therapeutic.

Your PT excursion also gives the floor nurses a break from you, and the Patient Representative time to rifle your room in search of Unapproved Substances such as food, your attorney's business card, and call-back messages from Geraldo.

## OCCUPATIONAL TERRORISTS

Occupational Therapists are there to teach you dandy little hints on Performing Daily Tasks in Your Weakened Condition, such as cutting your toenails, once you get out of the hospital.

In a fully equipped model kitchen, they will show you how to make dinner for your family while balanced on crutches and how to wash dishes without getting your home IV lines wet.

This is really helpful if your family is a bunch of lazy, insensitive slobs and you are dumber than a box of rocks for making them dinner in your Weakened Condition in the first place.

Just when you thought this hospital stint would buy you, oh, a good three weeks or so of lounging around the house with the remote control, here come the OTs, reminding you that you can do things for yourself! DO NOT LET THEM TALK TO YOUR FAMILY.

They have nifty Gadgets for Handicapped People, like 4-foot lobster claws with which you can grasp things from high shelves or low cupboards but which are best used for chasing away volunteers. They've got a carpenter's apron to wear or to tie to the front of your walker, so you can tote all your household cleaning supplies from room to room.

This is precisely what the average patient needs most—an undying hope, a cherished dream, an unwavering knowledge that, yes, as God is my witness, I WILL scrub lime deposits from the shower door again!

## TECHNICIANS

This is a catch-all term for anyone who Does Things To You.

You've got your lab technicians, your clinical technicians, your X-ray technicians, and your technical technicians. Many of the things they do are technical, hence the term *technician.*

Technicians fall into two groups: Malignant or Benign. Malignants perform hazardous and/or painful procedures, while Benigns perform Things You Don't Mind.

Most of the Malignants are located in the bowels of the building, because of the hazardous nature of the substances they work with, such as toxic waste and your diseased phlegm.

They are required by law to wear protective clothing such as you might see on "Lost in Space" to protect them from the substances to which they are going to freely expose you, like Agent Orange and radioactive particles.

Malignants are also the ones who perform the sorts of procedures that, if they were on film and sent through the mail, would get them 30 years in the federal pen. Working in hospitals productively channels their strange proclivities.

Benigns deal in more harmless procedures, such as taking your temperature. They no longer use normal glass thermometers with mercury and different-shaped tips to distinguish where they go. Apparently no one could remember which tip went where. They now use cake decorators that actually tell your temperature seconds after being stuck in your ear, ear wax being a very good conductor of heat.

The Benigns also do things like take your pulse, check your blood pressure, and run a pizza cutter across the soles of your feet to test your reflexes. (NOTE: This is not to be confused with cutting your toenails. If you believe a technician is attempting this unauthorized surgical procedure, notify Administration at once.)

They'll also give you a bed bath. They don't, however, do hair. Evidently the teeming mass of cooties setting up shop in the hair you haven't shampooed since you got there are Friendly Bacteria, like yogurt, and should not be disturbed.

# 4
# HOSPITAL FOOD

## AN OXYMORON

*Your meals will be brought to
you by people dressed, not
surprisingly, in the same sort
of decontamination outfits
worn by workers in biological-
warfare facilities.*

Your meals will be carefully planned by registered dietitians. (They are required by law to register, just like gun owners and convicted felons.)

Your menu will be selected and prepared to address your specific condition. For example, if you are nauseated, your entree will be the color and consistency of toad mucus and smell like a substandard nursing home.

This sophisticated technique is designed to speed the patient's own natural healing process by creating a compelling desire to leave the hospital as quickly as possible.

### YOUR FOUR BASIC FOOD GROUPS IN HOSPITALS

1. Your Slop Group
2. Your Mush Group
3. Your Petroleum Group
4. Your Sink-Clog Group

The highly trained dietary staff are experts in the art of culinary disguise. Leftover airline snacks and sludge from wastewater treatment facilities become tasty stews or creamy puddings.

(Actually, that is not entirely true. The meals are, of course, brought in by a pet food company.)

All food is tested for the presence of contaminants, such as flavor, and repeatedly washed and bleached so as to be hypo-allergenic.

If you are permitted to select your meals in advance from a preprinted menu, check off every item on the list and write in a few extra for good measure, like "salad bar" and "Sunday Brunch Buffet." Who knows? There might be someone new on duty who will send something edible by mistake.

As a general rule, avoid ordering anything that must be cooked or prepared, and don't EVER order organ meats in a hospital, for obvious reasons.

Your doctor may prescribe for you what's known as a "clear-liquid diet." This may bring back long-suppressed memories of that odd, Slavic babysitter who made you sip that bitter broth in the broom closet while listening to John Philip Sousa marches on the Victrola. However, the similarity is mere coincidence. The clear-liquid diet is nothing more than tepid water with oregano and air freshener and has no nutritional value.

· · · · · · · · · · · · · · · · · · · · · · · · · · · · · · · · · ·

## HANDY CULINARY TRANSLATIONS
## FOR READING THE MENU

Since Hospital Food and Real Food are two different things, you'll want to brush up on the following gastronomic euphemisms:

| HOSPITALESE | ENGLISH |
|---|---|
| Broth | Monkey urine |
| Scrambled eggs | Styrofoam packing peanuts |
| Fried eggs | Skin off the top of improperly sealed latex paint cans |
| Oatmeal | Elmer's School Glue |
| Baked chicken breast | Dr. Scholl's inserts |
| Lasagna | Leftovers from obstetrics |
| Beef stew | Ken-L-Ration |
| Meat loaf | "Whatever *did* happen to Lassie?" |
| Vegetable soup | Contents of the sink drainer |

· · · · · · · · · · · · · · · · · · · · · · · · · · · · · · · · · ·

| HOSPITALESE | ENGLISH |
|---|---|
| Apple juice | "Where's Mrs. Lieberman's specimen?" |
| Creamed corn | Creamed corn |
| Casserole | Chumming bait with extenders |
| Tapioca | Liposuction by-products |

Bon appétit.

# 5
# PROCEDURES AND DIAGNOSTIC TESTS

## YOUR LIFE AS A LABORATORY MOUSE

*A general rule of thumb is that
those orifices intended by
nature to let things out of the
body will now be used to put
things into the body, and vice
versa.*

Medical science is not content with the existing orifices of the human body and is intent on supplying more. This is the basis of many of your routine hospital procedures.

You will be asked to submit to practices similar to the rites of passage among tribesmen in remote Amazonian regions where human toes are the monetary unit.

Many patients believe that the Geneva Convention ensures protection from practices found in dusty reference books under the heading *Mengele, Dr.* This is foolish. The Geneva Convention mentions food, which hospitals are not prepared to provide.

## THE RELEASE OF LIABILITY

Before anything is perpetrated upon you, you will be required to sign a release the length of the U.S. Constitution and drafted by the lawyers who wrote the IRS 1040 Instruction Manual.

This is the only procedure for which you'll be heavily sedated.

The release acknowledges all 1,422 known risks and side effects, such as your brain exploding, and absolves anyone of any liability. It also releases the hospital from responsibility for those oh-so-human errors, such as criminal negligence.

After your sedation has taken effect, these forms will be shoved at you for your signature. If you manage to slur out some words meaning "I want to read this first," you will be given an icy stare meaning "Oh, great. Another ACLU lawyer." (Note: None of those people know what your signature looks like. Go ahead and sign it in the shakiest, most unreadable fashion possible. Hold the pen in the wrong hand. Misspell your name. If it ever comes up in court, it's evidence that you were clearly incapable of informed consent.)

A signed release is good for unlimited procedures and is taken to be valid until rescinded— sort of a medical Book-of-the-Month Club. Be sure to send in the postcard saying, "No, I do not want today's selection—*Coma*, by Robin Cook."

Sometimes your informed consent will be obtained verbally, although, of course, you will not remember it. Should you take issue with some procedure they have performed, such as having your spleen removed through your nose, they will gleefully remind you that you explicitly agreed to this, if you'll recall, just about the time you became incoherent from the morphine and Demerol shots.

## THE POOP POLICE

### A MOVEMENT FOR LAW AND ORDER

Hospitals are obsessed with your body's waste materials.

At first, you might find yourself a bit self-conscious about this. It's not something for which the average person aspiring to any social standing can prepare himself. One rarely invites the neighbors for dinner, videos, and a rousing discussion of waste products on display in mayonnaise jars in the den.

If you're one of those sensitive types who have difficulty with such matters, *get over it*—this stuff is going to be major news around the hospital. Because of the highly Medical Nature of fecal material, you will be interrogated frequently by highly trained experts known as the Poop Police. Many of them are former Nazi officers who can get anything out of anyone.

WARNING: DON'T EVER, EVER FLUSH WITHOUT PERMISSION FROM THE POOP PO- LICE! DESTROYING HARD EVIDENCE IS A SE- RIOUS OFFENSE.

They're particularly interested in your postop- erative poop. However, you'll be reluctant to ac- commodate them after surgery, since the process accurately simulates giving birth to Rosemary's Baby. In a wicker basket.

Give them what they want—or they'll DO things to you. Suffice it to say that you do not want them to DO things to you. Holding out on the Poop Police will buy you a history lesson in the ancient dyslexic fertility rite called The Enema.

## THE ENEMA

This procedure is administered by former gas station attendants who were fired for continuing to pump after the hose had clicked off.

It operates under the same premise as inducing vomiting by feeding you raw eggs, except that ingesting food through the mouth comes more naturally than drinking liquids with your behind. Consequently, your behind will be force-fed mass quantities of fluids by the use of tubes, WD-40, gravity, and pressure, all of which culminate in a disgusting mess and a lasting resolve to shove cat hair down the throat of the person who did this to you.

## THE URINE SQUAD

Working closely with the Poop Police is the Urine Squad, whose job it is to measure everyone's liquid output. We do not have all the details, but we think statistics are tabulated for the Chamber of Commerce, like annual rainfall, so as to attract toilet paper manufacturers to the city.

You will be asked, in genteel nurse terminology, to "pee" into a cardboard hat containing a ruler. These hats are made by people who lie to their friends about what they do for a living.

The hats are routinely collected by runners who record the results on a giant tote board, which is electronically linked to the New York Stock Exchange.

If you are incapable of a contribution, you will be assisted by a woman whose job credentials include three gold medals as a member of the former East German Olympic team and who was recruited through an ad in *Soldier of Fortune* magazine. This sturdy, hirsute angel of mercy will enter your room and, without warning, attempt to feed a garden hose into one of your smaller canals.

You'll be surprised how easily this feat is accomplished—with little more discomfort than passing a steel wool soap pad.

## A SAMPLING OF OTHER COMMON PROCEDURES

INJECTIONS. A medication is shot into your body by means of a needle jabbed into a vein or muscle. The technique is similar to Native American spear fishing or Haitian voodoo, depending upon the skill of the nurse.

The idea for this came from a now-extinct civilization whose members are believed to have all bled to death.

INTRAVENOUS TUBES (IVs). Turkey-trussing needles attached to refrigerator tubing are thrust into nerve-rich areas, such as the top of the hand, and left for extended periods. This procedure is performed by people whose hobbies include pithing frogs with letter openers.

TRACTION. Various limbs are attached to weights and pulleys until you confess to being a witch or a heretic.

CRYOTHERAPY. Ice is applied to painful areas, causing skin to become painfully cold, thereby drawing attention away from Actual Pain.

HYDROTHERAPY. This is the medical term for a nice hot bath. But they can't call it that because they can't charge you $175 for a nice hot bath. Since it often feels good (a violation of hospital policy), hydrotherapy is often coupled with freezing room temperatures.

WOUND IRRIGATION AND DRESSING CHANGES. Wounds and incisions are cleaned with substances that torture bacteria to death. Unfortunately, bacteria are very tiny, so they'll have to get this substance on you as well.

This will be done with the same gentle delicacy employed in tile-grout removal.

MANUAL INTERNAL EXAMS. This is much like a Punch and Judy show, wherein the doctor uses you as the hand puppet. He'll insert a gloved finger/hand/fist/arm into a body cavity and feel around for Things That Don't Feel Right. Of course, it won't feel right from your end, but that doesn't count.

Look carefully and you'll see that this glove is actually the Hamburger Helper Hand, sprayed with PAM. Note the smile on its little latex face.

The manual internal exam is performed in much the same way as one would vigorously clean out a turkey, except that feeling around for giblets is usually a more private affair than your typical internal exam.

Because of the inevitability of this exam at some point in your life, it's an important consideration when selecting a doctor. Note the size of his hands. Can he palm a basketball? Do his fingers resemble huge carrots fed with Miracle-Gro?

## ANESTHETICS

Doctors view anesthetics as inadvisable, since they consider it beneficial for you to be able to alert them to any teensy errors, such as the severing of your spinal cord.

In rare cases, you will grudgingly be given relaxants or painkillers for a particularly excruciating procedure, such as those involving power drills and soldering irons.

Actually, the term "painkillers" is a misnomer. They don't actually *stop* pain. They only suppress your ability to *express* that pain by paralyzing your vocal cords. These are primarily for the benefit of staff.

Other "painkillers" actually induce amnesia. You feel the pain in all its intensity—you just repress it until the doctors have moved to affluent resort communities in different time zones.

## TESTS, TESTS, AND MORE TESTS

You will be taken frequently to remote parts of the hospital for Secret, Mysterious Tests, much like those experienced by Arkansas farmers kidnapped by extraterrestrials.

You will be studied for the survival of their species. They will tell you that they are friendly and come in peace, that they mean you no harm. (The basic creed of doctors is, in fact, *Primum,*

*non nocecere,* which means "First, do no harm."
Coincidence? Perhaps. Ever notice how they all
wear gloves? Could it be that their hands *aren't
like ours?*)

## RULES OF DIAGNOSTIC TESTING

*1. Patients must fast for forty days and forty nights
before a test.*

This ensures that your tests will uncover a
Medical Condition, such as malnutrition and dehy-
dration.

A large sign will be posted on your door: DO
NOT GIVE THIS PATIENT ANY FOOD OR
DRINK. This is, of course, nonsense—there is no
actual food in a hospital.

Withholding fluids serves no medical function, except to amuse the staff as they watch the
zany antics of parched, dehydrated patients lick-
ing the condensation off the windows.

*2. You may be required to ingest something prior
to a test.*

This, of course, will not be food or drink as
we know it; rather, you will be forced to eat or
drink something that, if consumed *outside* the
hospital, would put you *in* the hospital.

For example, you may be given a plastic con-
tainer (which looks suspiciously like a specimen
cup) full of tub caulking to drink. DON'T DO IT!!
This is a test to see how stupid you are.

The real drink is made from baby powder and

Mazola, mixed with hazardous waste from nuclear power plants.

3. *The results of all diagnostic tests must indicate the need for further diagnostic tests.*

First, you will be tested to see if you can withstand testing. This test, along with the results of your Dun & Bradstreet report, determines your tolerance level for risk, pain, humiliation, and expense, so that they know how many tests to perform.

Since everything being done to you can cause side effects that produce abnormal test results, none of the tests can ever be conclusive and must therefore be repeated forever.

4. *The distance you must travel, and the ruggedness of the terrain, is in direct proportion to your level of pain.*

If you're in severe pain, you'll be bounced through construction zones with crude ramps and loud jackhammers. (Hospitals, like Chicago expressways, are always under construction.)

5. *Proper preparation for diagnostic tests includes extended periods of abandonment in deserted hallways and/or public areas.*

You will be left On Display in various stages of undress and disarray for the amusement of visitors and staff, as an example of how extremely busy this hospital is.

Or, without warning you will be parked in a makeshift walkway, consisting of plastic sheeting and canvas flaps, between two buildings and deserted by the attendant for several hours.

6. *The hallway in which you are parked must have careful climate control.*

If it is summer, the hallway will be the approximate temperature of melted glass.

If it is winter, frigid winds in excess of 60 miles per hour will whip through like a wind tunnel, and ice crystals will form in your IV bag. (This is a dangerous condition requiring immediate medical attention. Make an appointment to see your doctor as soon as possible.)

## BLOOD TESTS

For centuries, leeches provided a simple, painless method for obtaining blood. But they were annoying to sterilize, became inordinately attached to the patients, and were dismissed as barbaric. Science searched for a compassionate alternative. A four-inch steel needle was the obvious choice.

Since there are 15,742 profitable tests that can be run on your blood, you'll become intimately familiar with a ritual known as Finding a Vein. This entails cutting off the circulation with a rubber hose such as you'd find in black-and-white gangster movies.

You will be informed that you have terrible veins. This puts the blame for any mistakes squarely where it belongs—on you. At 20-minute intervals you'll be jabbed, and any blood in the vicinity will be removed.

This will leave you in a Weakened Condition, requiring a transfusion from supplies Contaminated in Statistically Insignificant Amounts. More blood will be drawn just to confirm the statistical insignificance.

Eventually, all your veins will collapse and they'll be forced to use unsterilized leeches.

### CAT SCAN

This test transmits a computerized image of your soft tissues onto a TV screen. This is much like PBS or the Discovery Channel in that this is educational rather than entertaining.

You will be put into a machine similar to the ones featured on the Home Shopping Network that turn out enormous loaves of tasty French bread. It does, however, require absolute stillness on your part, rendering it impractical for use on live patients.

### CARDIAC CATHETERIZATION

In a bizarre twist on the old saying "The quickest way to a man's heart is through his stomach," a catheter is inserted into an artery in—get this—*your arm, leg, or groin* and guided up and around and over and under until it gets to your . . . *heart!*

This is medical proof of what women have known for years: the quickest way to a man's heart is through his groin.

You'll receive only a worthless sedative, such as Pez, so that you may fully experience this festive moment—and also alert the doctor to any wrong turns resulting in death.

The complexity of this procedure is best understood by removing the drawstring from your sweatpants and placing the pants and string inside an arcade game. Now, with the mechanical arms, rethread the drawstring into the waistband.

## CYSTOMETRY

This test was invented by a deranged child left alone for extended periods of time with only her Betsy Wetsy doll for company.

For this test, a tube is inserted into your tiniest orifice by a member of the Urine Squad. The diameter of the tube is always precisely twice that of the orifice and, for the best effect, is often corrugated.

Then your bladder is pumped full of water to see how much it can hold before you become homicidal. For additional fun, your bladder is alternately filled with hot and cold water and your reaction is recorded for "America's Funniest Home Videos."

## EKG

With an EKG, which measures heart activity, a dozen or so self-adhesive disks with wires attached to a machine are super-glued to your chest, arms, and feet.

When the disks are removed, they'll take along any hair carelessly left in the area. It's uncomfortable only if you have a hairy chest of the sort which encourages animal nesting.

The Stress EKG is the same procedure plus a treadmill that can be set to various speeds, including "Heart Attack." This allows you to have your heart attack under optimal conditions, where you can be promptly treated—and probably saved.

## ENDOSCOPY

Endoscopy is a general term for any procedure where the doctor inserts a periscope inside you via an existing or newly created opening in your body and browses about your internal organs from the comfort of his own office.

There are a whole bunch of tests employing this method:

BRONCHOSCOPY. This is a pleasant little test invented by a group of frat brothers after a rousing night of pledge hazing.

First, your tongue will be wrapped in gauze and your throat sprayed with a disgusting liquid to calm your gag reflex. It will take effect after you stop vomiting.

Then, you swallow a snorkel.

The doctor will help by pushing it down through your windpipe and into your lungs. This snorkel has a light, a camera lens, and a whirling brush; it was originally intended for use aboard the *Calypso*.

Once the snorkel is stuffed in, you'll experience the sensation of being unable to breathe. You'll then panic and try to rip the doctor's face off, which he finds highly annoying, because of course you really *can* breathe if you just calm down and quit acting as if you had a snorkel stuffed down your throat.

If you're a sword swallower by trade, this is a breeze.

COLANGIOPANCREATOGRAPHY (ERCP). Bronchoscopy and more!

For this test, you will be blindfolded so that you cannot identify anyone who did this to you. Then you will be sedated just enough so that you are not a credible witness.

The periscope/snorkel is passed (guided, eased, shoved) through your throat and esophagus, all the way down to your stomach and small intestine in total disregard for the Geneva Convention.

Dye is shot into a catheter in the scope, and you're then positioned like Gumby for lovely color X-rays. If they see something they don't like in there, they may just go ahead and yank it out with the periscope/snorkel, which comes equipped with grappling hooks for just such an occasion.

When the test is complete, the doctors and nurses will receive new identities from the Federal Witness Protection Program.

COLONOSCOPY, or PROCTOSIGMOIDOSCOPY. These tests, invented by inmates of a correctional institution, involve snaking an instrument through—are you ready for this?—up to *five feet* of your lower intestinal tract.

You are asked to assume an extremely embarrassing position, such as you might use to moon the ceiling. You will be left that way for about an hour to wait for the doctor. This is a crude attempt at anesthesia, whereby the freezing room temperatures will numb your behind. (Hence, the term "blue moon.")

After you and the doctor exchange niceties about the weather, he makes access through an opening normally reserved for activities involving toilet paper and a good book. Much to your delight, a vacuum cleaner hose, equipped with lights and cameras, is pushed through your personal plumbing. This is known as "cramming for the test."

The hose will then be hooked up to a leaf blower until you resemble a Macy's Parade balloon. They'll tell you that if you are relaxed, this test won't cause much discomfort. Of course, they're criminally insane and habitual liars.

CYSTOURTHROSCOPY. The idea for this came from a group of deviant PBX operators.

It employs the best of cystometry and endoscopy: you get not one but *two* things inserted into your smallest canal.

First, you'll be searched for any weapons that might be used for retaliation. Then, a urethroscope goes in. (This is actually an uncooked manicotti shell.) Then a cystoscope (too medical to describe) goes into your bladder and you're pumped full of sterile medical waste. Observations are made, such as "Look at how her eyes are bulging!" and "Patient has now bitten completely through his lower lip."

When the test is completed, you may resume normal activities, such as psychotherapy, heavy drinking, and planning the doctor's demise.

GI (GASTROINTESTINAL) SERIES. This diagnostic test comes in two varieties—Upper and Lower. If you have a choice, select the Upper.

With the Upper GI Series, you'll be forced to swallow barium, a vile liquid concoction used as gravy on hospital food. Like all substances found in Superfund landfills, it shows up well on X-rays.

With the Lower GI Series, the process is the same, except that you don't have to drink the barium. Good, right?

Wrong. First, they sell tickets. Then they pump the stuff into your behind with a bicycle pump, followed up with air from a fireplace bellows. You'll be tilted upside down to slosh the barium around. Then they'll take pictures, which will be passed around at the radiologists' Christmas party.

(This test is performed by only the most experienced technicians. Keeping a straight face takes years of practice.)

## MRI (MAGNETIC RESONANCE IMAGING)

Doctors love this test because (a) it permits them to view your soft tissues without endangering themselves by getting near you while you are radioactive, and (b) it's very expensive.

Instead of radiation, the MRI machine uses a strong magnetic field. Passersby with extensive dental work frequently must be pried from the side of the machine with a crowbar.

You'll be put into a large sarcophagus, which gives you a feel for what it's like to be an ancient dead Egyptian. They'll slam the hatch shut and scatter for the exits.

You will then hear loud, banging noises. Several dozen crazed trolls, of the sort you'd find under bridges, are hammering away with mallets and axes, trying to deafen you. After about 45 minutes they'll tire of this sport and scurry off to harass someone else.

The test will, of course, be declared inconclusive because you moved, and the lucrative process will have to be repeated.

## MAMMOGRAM

This is an X-ray that has its own name because no one wants to actually say the word *breast.*

Mammograms require your breast to do gymnastics. If you have extremely agile breasts, you should do fine. Most breasts, however, pretty much hang around doing nothing in particular, so they're woefully unprepared.

But you can prepare for a mammogram right at home, using these simple exercises:

EXERCISE 1. Refrigerate two bookends overnight. Lay one of your breasts (either will do) between the two bookends and smash the bookends together as hard as you can. Repeat three times daily.

EXERCISE 2. Locate a pasta maker or old wringer washer. Feed the breast into the machine and start cranking. Repeat twice a day.

EXERCISE 3 (Advanced). Situate yourself comfortably on your side on the garage floor. Place one of your breasts snugly behind the rear tire of the family van. When you give the signal, hubby will slowly ease the car into reverse. Hold for five seconds. Repeat on the other side.

## NUCLEAR SCANNING

Developed by doctors in Hiroshima and Chernobyl, these tests use radioactive substances to make your insides glow in the dark.

You will be assured that these substances are only hazardous if encountered in Real Life on unwashed apples belonging to Meryl Streep or on restricted Army bases in New Mexico. Deliberate radiation is apparently safer than plain radiation.

Besides, you'll be exposed to such low doses that it hardly pays to think about it. (Which is why they lock you into a lead-lined room and scatter like cockroaches, monitoring you through specially insulated glass as if you were microwave popcorn.)

Radioactivity can also be injected *directly into your bloodstream.* This reduces the chance of these completely harmless particles getting on your doctor and causing him to grow gills.

You'll then be scanned by a machine to determine which organs are radioactive and should therefore be removed.

## PROSTATE EXAM

For an accurate depiction of this exam, rent the movie *Deliverance.*

## X-RAYS

To doctors, everything is a photo opportunity.

Using rays emitted from dying galaxies, technicians capture on film those tender, wacky internal Kodak moments we all experience, such as ruptures, fractures, and lesions.

They are trained to pose you in positions you never thought possible outside of carnival midways and page 57 of the Kama Sutra. You'll be placed directly in contact with the photographic plate, which is stored in the vegetable crisper of the fridge.

They may call in Special Effects to get artsy and inject you with a contrast medium. This is similar to the way florists make blue carnations—except that flowers don't have nerve endings and blue food coloring does not appear on the periodic table.

Aside from accumulation of radioactivity in your body, to levels such as those found in soil samples on ranches where cattle are mysteriously dying, X-rays pose little danger.

## ULTRASOUND

Sound waves are bounced off your insides and show up on a TV screen in the manner employed in *The Hunt for Red October.*

The technician smears a cold, jellylike glop onto the area to be visualized. Then she runs a chilled microphone over the area until your insides are projected on a monitor.

As diagnostic tests go, this is the one to have. There's no pain (or, to use medical terminology, no *discomfort*). Nothing is shoved into you, and there's no radiation. The biggest hazard is having your liver mistaken for a Russian sub.

# 6
# SURGERY

## THE CUTTING EDGE OF HEALTH CARE

*Surgery is both a science and
an art. One can only hope that
art imitates life. The art of
surgery is best done in the
school of realism. Beware of
abstract, primitive, and surreal
art.*

## AN OVERVIEW

Surgery is anything that involves cutting you open for the purpose of removing, adding, or tinkering with your parts.

It is much like auto repair, except that getting the transmission overhauled in your Volvo is a lot cheaper, and your insurance company won't raise your rates for having your car fixed.

There are two basic kinds of surgery—Minor and Major. The distinction between the two is determined by cost and whether it is being done *by* the doctor or *to* the doctor. There are six subcategories:

1. Emergency Surgery. Your condition demands immediate attention. Examples include being impaled on a flag pole or swallowing a hand grenade. Do not bother with a second opinion.

2. Urgent Surgery. Condition requires prompt attention within the next day or two. Tumors large enough to require a separate airline ticket fall into this category.

3. Required Surgery. Conditions indicate you gotta have it, but no hurry. "You gotta have it" means different things to different doctors, depending on their skill, experience, and bank account. A second opinion might shoot you down to the next category.

4. Elective Surgery. You should be operated on, but what the hey? This category includes bunions. (If, however, your bunions slice open your

shoes and lacerate passersby, go back one space to Required Surgery.)

5. Optional Surgery. This is your Cher, Michael Jackson, and Mafia-informant category.

6. Unnecessary Surgery. This is surgery performed on healthy body parts for obscure reasons known only to the doctor and his accountant. It is never performed on doctors and very rarely on contingency lawyers—by mistake.

## ROUTINE SURGERY

All surgeries will be described as "routine." This should not be equated with *your* routine, which includes watching Monday Night Football with a six-pack of beer. What is meant is the *doctor's* routine, wherein he fillets people on a daily basis with no actual discomfort to himself.

## PREPARATION FOR SURGERY

Regardless of the type of surgery you will have, preparation is essentially the same:
- Examination: Your insurance card and checkbook will be thoroughly examined. If either shows signs of anemia, surgery will be postponed until they're healthy and can survive the trauma.
- Shaving: No matter what is being operated on, you'll be shaved. If your private areas are involved, the public will be invited. If there is no hair in the vicinity of the pro-

posed incision, they'll select another, *hairier*, surgical site.

- Enema: While not always a medical necessity, the enema is now tradition. Prep nurses have so little opportunity for frivolity. So, even if you're in for cataracts, expect the Roto-Rooter.

- Fasting: You will not be given anything to eat or drink for 24 hours before surgery, since hospital food will cause you to throw up and obscure the surgeon's vision. Fasting is also a diagnostic test. If you survive, you're strong enough for surgery.

- Sedatives and narcotics: An hour or two before surgery, you'll be given enough drugs to make you incoherent, yet entertaining. This lets them get you to the operating room with a minimum of fuss, because you think you're lying naked on the buffet table at the office Christmas party, an activity you happen to like.

- Stomach tubes: Just in case the fasting and the enema missed a corn niblet, a tube will be passed into your stomach to suck it out. This tube goes in through your nose, down your throat, and into your stomach, and is no more unpleasant than inhaling an eel. Your nasal passages and throat will be raw and painful later, but you'll hardly notice because you will be distracted by your painful surgical wounds.

- Urinary catheter: Because it is so annoying

for surgeons to have to stop what they're doing while you get up to go to the bathroom, they prefer to siphon this stuff out of you. This is usually done before you are anesthetized so they can see the look on your face.

• Intravenous infusions: Because of all the diagnostic tests and fasting—not to mention the fact that there's something wrong with you—you're likely to have lousy blood chemistry. So they'll pump you full of vitamins, minerals, Ovaltine, and Tang to make you strong. This will be done via (surprise!) tubes in your veins.

## ON TO THE OPERATING ROOM!

*The operating room* is stark, cold, and uninviting and could be much improved with the addition of some rich floral fabrics and parlor palms. As it is, it looks much like the bathroom of a new subway system.

*The operating table* itself is cold, hard, and quite narrow, with room for only one person. Ask for a goose-down quilt.

*The lighting* is extremely harsh and unflattering. This leads doctors to think you are far too unattractive to be bothered by large, disfiguring scars. This relieves them of the pressure to be neat, and speeds up the whole process.

*The instrument table* contains all the tools needed to open, tinker, remove, repair, or replace your body parts. DO NOT LOOK AT THIS TABLE!! There is no need to see the Skil-Saw, Swiss Army knife, serrated grapefruit spoon, vise, hatchet, and machete.

*The solution basins* are placed around the table for discarded instruments, much like the buckets provided at seafood restaurants for shells. There are also solution buckets the surgeon can dunk his hands into if there is too much of you on him.

*The waste buckets* on the floor are for used gauze, sponges, and any internal organs left over after you're put back together. In the rural South, these also serve as spittoons.

*Monitors* record your vital signs, letting the surgeon know how you're doing and if it's worth his while to be tidy.

## THE FINAL COUNTDOWN

Members of the surgical team will be dressed like contestants on a game show that features seltzer and whipped cream in its stunts.

They will be wearing motel shower caps on their heads and feet, long green gowns, Hamburger Helper gloves, and masks to conceal their identity.

A surgical nurse will thoroughly scrub the area to be operated on. This area is called the surgical "field." If she called it by its real name— say Marilyn or Charles—she might choke and say, "Ohmigod, what are we doing?"

She will scrub the area raw and then paint it Day-Glo Orange so the surgeon can spot it right off the bat. The rest of your body will be draped with sheets to disguise you.

You'll be restrained with straps, ostensibly to protect you from touching the sterile field. Actually, this is done to prevent you from deliberately tearing off the surgeon's testicles.

## ANESTHESIA

The term *anesthesia* was first used by Oliver Wendell Holmes, whose son of the same name grew up to be a lawyer, which is reason enough to want to be put to sleep.

If you were born before 1846, you will remember when the typical anesthesia consisted of lashing the patient to a tree while the attending physician drank Scotch and wore ear plugs.

Then came modern science, which over the past 150 years has developed astounding techniques to keep the patient quiet so the surgeon needs only a small amount of Scotch.

Today, the doctor who administers the anesthesia is called the anesthesiologist—as opposed to centuries ago, when he was called the bartender.

The anesthesiologist charges great sums of money to put you to sleep, which the chaplain and the volunteers will do for free. After you're asleep, he'll shove an airway in your throat and whisper subliminal messages, like "Pay me great sums of money."

Just kidding. They hardly ever put you to sleep.

Now that medical science has given us all of these miraculous anesthetics, lawyers have discovered that it is dangerous to give them to you. So the anesthesiologist is there only to hold that mask over your face to stifle your screams.

Local or regional anesthesia is preferable so that you are awake and alert to fully appreciate the difficulty of the procedure, which will be apparent from the sounds of crunching and tearing. You will be informed that the pain you are feeling is merely pressure.

(Note: There is no anesthesia for the procedure known as Administering the Local Anesthesia, since the pain is of short duration and not much worse than stapling your tongue to a brick.)

*On occasion*, they will put you totally under. This is done with a combination of injected drugs and inhaled gases. The gases are collected from the exhaust pipes of Greyhound buses or live volcanos and are stored in tanks marked, "DANGER!! HIGHLY FLAMMABLE," which is the internationally recognized code for "Safe to Breathe."

Your skin color is an accurate gauge of how you're responding to these noxious gases. Consequently, all makeup and fingernail polish must be removed. There have been many tragic cases involving circus clowns and televangelists' wives who might have been saved if only the anesthesiologist had been able to see that they had turned blue.

# LIGHTS! CAMERA! ACTION! CUT!

There are many different types of surgery, all of which are pretty gruesome affairs. Unfortunately, space restrictions prohibit a detailed account of what actually takes place in the operating room.

The reader is directed to the following reference materials for more complete information:

- *Field Dressing a Deer: A Step-by-Step Guide*
- *The Whole House Plumbing Manual*
- *Old World Artisan Guide to Whittling and Woodburning*
- *Fun With Ginsu Knives: The Art of Bonsai and Deboning Chicken*

Following surgery, the surgeon will sew you up. This is not the place to cut costs. Resist the temptation to save with the "Autopsy Close-Up Special," which uses marlin line. Many patients find that a petit-point rendition of "Home Sweet Home" across their bellies is well worth the additional charge.

# POSTOPERATIVE

After you have recovered from surgery and have been brought back to your room, you will experience some aftereffects.

For example, you will begin plotting the painful, slow death of the family doctor who talked you into this. This is natural and healthy and will distract you from your other postoperative symptoms, which include:

- Nausea and vomiting. Since you've fasted, had an enema, and swallowed stomach tubes to clear you out completely, you might be puzzled as to how this can happen. It appears that during surgery your body manufactures partially digested corn, peas, and Oreo cookies for just such an occasion.
- Pain. Pain is a medically desirable aftereffect of surgery. Doctors realize that the desire for revenge is a powerful motivator in regaining one's strength.

    Each patient reacts differently to pain. Some patients deal with pain through the use of colorful language, wherein everyone within earshot learns new, creative things to do to themselves with various objects.

    You may be given pain medication, as described in Chapter 5. This will make you incoherent, and you will say things like "Billy me albatross on Bullwinkle four Fig Newtons." Of course, you'll still be fully aware of the pain, but no one else will know it. This makes everyone feel much better, especially the staff, who now feel free to do Unpleasant Things to You since you're not in pain.
- Dizziness and weakness. This is perfectly normal and is actually helpful to your re-

covery. It is nature's way of telling you that you have just been laid open like a flounder. If you didn't feel so weak, you might do something to break open your stitches, like aerobics or calf roping.

## POSTOPERATIVE ACTIVITIES

### WALKING

As soon as you've stopped throwing up, they will get you out of bed and make you walk. This is the Lazarus therapy used in the Bible, and it worked quite well for him. You, however, might have a little more trouble.

Don't bother with the whining and protests; they've heard it all. So what if you just came out of surgery? That's no excuse. Walking is good for you, especially when it's slow and painful.

They'll gather up all the tubes, wires, monitors, and bags for you to drag along. You'll then inch your way down the road to recovery at a rate of 1 FTPH (floor tile per hour), using the IV pole for support. You'll continue until you catch a glimpse of your reflection and fall into a heap on the floor.

This process will be repeated several times a day until you are well enough to be released, at which time you will be made to ride in a wheelchair to the car.

## EATING

If you are hungry and thirsty, you will not be allowed food or drink. Instead, you will be fed intravenously. If you have no appetite, you will be *made* to eat what is loosely defined as food, in the form of mysterious broths and watery puddings.

In a few days you will be put on a regimen of regular hospital food, which often eliminates the need for a postoperative enema.

## COUGHING

Coughing in Real Life usually means you are sick and should see a doctor. However, coughing in the hospital is Therapeutic and is encouraged. They are adamant about this.

Of course, this is the last thing you want to do after surgery. You're not stupid. You saw *Alien*, and you're well aware of what it's like to have your chest explode.

Nevertheless, you'll be coached in the art of coughing. You will be given a little airline pillow to hold against you, which will supposedly make this a painless affair. You will gingerly expel a tiny puff of air. This, of course, does not satisfy the Cough Coach. She wants you to take a deep breath and HACK. To which you respond, "I'll see you in hell first."

COMPLICATIONS

Ever vigilant and acutely aware of Things That
Can Go Wrong, your medical team will be on the
alert for signs of complications. The following
symptoms are a signal that you may be experiencing postoperative complications:

- Your breathing sounds like you're making
  cappuccino.
- Your heart rate mimics the Dow Jones In-
  dustrial Average.
- Your catheters begin showing hard-water
  stains.
- Your incision resembles improperly refrig-
  erated ground beef.
- You begin coughing up fur balls.

"Now this won't hurt a bit."

# 7
# SPEAKING THE LANGUAGE

## BILINGUALISM: A CHRONIC CONDITION

*Rules of Grammar: Notice that the pronouns "you" and "I" do not exist in Hospitalese, having been replaced with* we. *The only exception to this rule: "<u>You</u> are responsible for the hospital bill."*

As with any visit to a foreign country, you'll find your stay much richer if you speak at least some of the language. The natives will not necessarily be flattered, as they would be in Spain or Mississippi, but knowing a few key phrases in Hospitalese will help you get around.

Hospitalese is confusing because it utilizes English words, but these words do not mean the same thing as they do in English.

For example, the English word *unpleasant*, conveys a sense of mild annoyance. In Hospitalese, however, the word *unpleasant* means "humiliating, painful," and, occasionally, "deviant."

. . . . . . . . . . . . . . . . . . . . . . . . . . . . . . . . .

## TRANSLATIONS

Handy phrases for unschooled cretins who wish
to understand trained medical personnel:

| HOSPITALESE | ENGLISH |
|---|---|
| Doctor's orders | I have no idea what this is and why I'm giving it to you, so shut up. |
| Mild discomfort | Really painful |
| Some discomfort | *#!@$& |
| Uncomfortable | Did you ever see *Texas Chainsaw Massacre?* |
| You'll feel a little stick. | Spear dipped in curare |
| Just a little sting | Army ants and killer bees |
| Try to relax. | Get your fingernails out of my arm. |
| This might feel a little cool. | Remember that winter your tongue got stuck on the window? |
| You'll feel a little tug. | Tractor pull |
| Try to get some rest. | Quit with the call button, already! |

. . . . . . . . . . . . . . . . . . . . . . . . . . . . . . . . .

· · · · · · · · · · · · · · · · · · · · · · · · · · · · · · · · · · ·

| HOSPITALESE | ENGLISH |
|---|---|
| You're looking better. | Norman Bates's mother propped up in bed |
| We've ordered more tests. | You have excellent insurance. |
| Can I get you anything? | Water? Sherbet? A muzzle? |
| It's just routine. | They do this stuff all the time in POW camps. |

· · · · · · · · · · · · · · · · · · · · · · · · · · · · · · · · · · ·

## TECHNICAL HOSPITALESE, OR MEDICALESE

Much of the technical form of Hospitalese is based on Latin, a language the Italians scrapped centuries ago in favor of one they could understand—namely, Italian.

Doctors favor this language because it makes them sound powerful, like the Pope, and keeps patients from understanding them.

To further reduce any chance of outsiders comprehending their secret language, doctors have peppered it with ancient Greek. This is a language spoken by now-deceased men with leaves in their hair who wore bedsheets and wrote plays about people who ate their children.

The technical, Latin/Greek dialect of Hospitalese, known as Medicalese, is also useful when it comes to charging you vast sums of money. *Contusions* are much more costly than *bruises.* It is also much easier to make things up using this dialect, since no one knows what the hell it means, except the Pope and Alex Karras. ("Could be a case of venividivici, with complications of the mea culpa Euripides hydra.")

### BRIEF GLOSSARY OF MEDICALESE

With little or no training, and these simple terms, you too can sound like a medical doctor!

**Etiology**, n., cause or origin. From the Latin *eti,* meaning, "I have eaten," and *ology,* meaning "study of." Hence, the cause of a disease, since you are what you eat—as in, "an ulcer of burrito etiology."

**Idiopathic**, adj., "I don't know." From the Latin *idio,* meaning, "I am an idiot," and *patho,* meaning "pathetic." As in "I think your disease was idiopathic, but I might be wrong."

**Pathology**, n., abnormality. From the Greek *patho,* meaning, "pathetic," and *lodge,* meaning "Nixon's running mate in 1960."

**Psychosomatic**, adj., "You're nuts." From the Greek *psycho,* meaning, "Anthony Perkins dressed as his mother," and *soma,* meaning, "So what?" As in "You have a psychosomatic pathology of idiopathic etiology, but who cares?"

## MEDICALESE SELF-TAUGHT

Many other impressive Medicalese phrases can be formed by simply combining beginnings and ends of ancient words. They are interchangeable, much like Garanimals. Examine the following definitions and create your own genuine Medical Terms!

| PREFIX | WHAT IT MEANS | SUFFIX | WHAT IT MEANS |
|--------|---------------|--------|---------------|
| ecto- | outside | -osis | disease |
| neur- | nerve | -itis | inflammation |
| pneum- | air | -ectomy | cutting out |
| mal- | bad | -algia | pain in |
| macro- | large | -otomy | cutting into |
| myel- | spine; backbone | -emia | blood |
| gastr- | stomach | -asia | formation |
| derm- | skin | | |
| post- | after; behind | | |
| hypo- | deficient; weak | | |

Examples:

*Postalgia*—pain in the butt, as in "The patient in 352 is giving me postalgia."

*Ectopostdermatitis*—hemorrhoids, as in "His ectopostdermatitis flares up when he eats sunflower seeds with the shells on."

*Macroneurosis*—a lot of nerve, as in "You've got macroneurosis if you think you're going to stick that thing in me."

*Macrogastrotomy*—belt is too tight, as in "After Thanksgiving dinner, the patient suffered acute macrogastrotomy."

*Hypomyelosis*—cowardice, as in "He'll need anesthesia during surgery due to acute hypomyelosis."

*Malpneumopostasia*—flatulence, as in "Whew! Better get some Air Wick, honey. The patient in 16B with the idiopathic burrito etiology has got a serious case of malpneumopostasia."

See how easy this is?

# 8
# HOSPITAL FASHION

## FEELING LIKE HELL
## IS NO EXCUSE FOR LOOKING LIKE IT

*During your hospitalization, a
time when you will be
receiving more visitors than
the Smithsonian, you will look
like something the puppy
coughed up.*

## FASHION DOS AND DON'TS

***DON'T*** *wear the standard-issue hospital gown.*

It will mark you as an emergency room admission, an indigent, or a complete weenie with incredibly bad taste.

Designed by the creators of plaster-elf lawn ornaments, the hospital gown was originally intended for use as a barbecue apron in rural trailer parks.

Today, all hospital gowns are custom-tailored to the individual patient by the same people who make one-size-fits-all panty hose. It is illegal for these gowns to meet in the back.

***DO*** *bring along a pillowcase to wear over your head.*

If you must wear a hospital gown, a simple yet elegant pillowcase slipped over the face will hide your identity and shield you from the embarrassment caused by your exposed parts.

***DO*** *select camouflaging bedwear.*

Women find that blinding shades of neon draw attention away from pallid, chalky complexions and other beauty hazards associated with disease. Dizzying patterns help disguise stains from pesky spurting veins, draining wounds, and the vomit-related mishaps associated with hospital meals.

*DO select two-piece pajama sets in a subdued plaid or seersucker, preferably monogrammed.*

This will mark you men as conservative, no-nonsense types with access to a battery of contingency lawyers. Speedo trunks and a tank top emblazoned with the words "Chick Magnet" ensure that finding a vein will become a lengthy, painful ordeal.

*DO bring a floor-length robe.*

Female patients will want to cover their pasty, stubble-studded legs. Male patients, unless they're pro athletes, will want to hide their legs even after they're out of the hospital.

You'll want this coverage for times when you're in a wheelchair being paraded through the visitor's lounge and onto the public elevator (which always serves a 50-story office building as well as the hospital) with your bedwear hiked up to your waist.

*DO tuck tweezers into your overnight bag.*

Remember, you'll be lying on your back. People will be seeing you from above, with a good view up your nose and an excellent angle on that single wiry black hair growing out of the mole underneath your chin.

*DON'T wear the hospital-issued underwear.*

These are one-size-fits-all stretch-mesh monstrosities such as European peasants use for carrying produce from the market. They will leave imprints on your backside that look as if you've been sitting on a waffle iron.

## BEAUTY AND GROOMING

Personal grooming during periods of intense physical pain or drugged stupor is often difficult, which is why sick people frequently look so terrible. You will see them being escorted about as a sadistic reminder of what you now look like: a feebleminded soul whose picture appears in newspaper ads at holiday time with the caption, "Won't you help?"

### HAIR

The only thing the hospital staff is allowed to do to your hair is shave it. So unless you're in for brain surgery, looking good is going to be a problem.

Your unwashed hair will be matted with sebum and perspiration and pasted flat against the back of your head from lying in bed. It will stick straight out on one side and straight up on top, giving you the look of a seriously demented chicken.

You will then be wheeled about the hospital and displayed to the General Public, who will gawk and wave as if you were this year's Senile Dementia float in the Rose Parade. Most of these onlookers have never been hospitalized and there-fore assume that you look like that because you are criminally insane.

You may be given a small bottle of no-rinse shampoo, which supposedly washes your hair without water. This is a lie. If you spray this stuff in your hair, what you get is hair crawling with the same dirt, oils, sweat, dead skin cells, airborne viruses, and bacon bits—plus sticky no-rinse shampoo gunk.

### HELPFUL HINTS FOR BEAUTIFUL HAIR

- Before entering the hospital, have your stylist give you a no-care, stylish cut. Bring in magazine pictures of stars with the look you want. Good choices: Sinead O'Connor, Telly Savalas, and Vanessa Redgrave in her role as Joan of Arc.
- Emergency room admission? No time for a new "do"? Here's how to perk up even the most lifeless, filthy hair after a week of thrashing about in bed: Plop a bar of soap into your bedside water pitcher. In an hour or so, dump it over your head. A Senior Citizen Trying To Stay Active is bound to show up in a matter of minutes with your rinse water.
- If you color your hair, have the roots touched up before your hospital stay. It's bad enough looking weak, pallid, and pathetic. Don't add *cheap floozie*.

- If you were an emergency room admission with no time for root touch-ups or a trim, now's the time for that pillowcase.
- Wigs and toupees are a last-ditch option, but only if you want to look like a TV evangelist with a ferret on your head.
- Hats cover your unsightly hair while keeping crows from nesting and weaving in bits of tin foil from your dinner tray. Avoid novelty hats with beer cans or phrases like "Shit Happens."

## A WORD ABOUT SHAVING

Unless you're feeling pretty perky, shaving is not going to be part of your daily grooming routine.

In hospitals, shaving is for surgical preparation only and is reserved for areas of the body where you *want* hair, such as your scalp and your private areas.

Keeping you unshaven also serves a tactical purpose. It's harder for patients to be assertive and businesslike when they look like derelict winos.

## BATHING

If you are unable to get to the bathroom, you will be given a bed bath. Technicians will very conscientiously wash all those parts that get so filthy while lying in bed doing nothing, like your elbows and your knees.

They'll sponge down your hands and arms and feet, taking care not to cut themselves on your now-lethal toenails. Then they'll hand you the washcloth so you can cleanse your own Private Parts while they pretend to avert their eyes in amusement.

Conversation is likely to be strained at this point. Dogs are nonchalant about this and would perform their personal hygiene on C-Span. You, however, will act as if you've been caught at something, such as sponging your private parts.

## CALLING DR. LAUDER . . . DR. ESTEE LAUDER . . .

Wearing makeup in the hospital is like spray-painting dead shrubbery green: it looks really, really stupid and only draws attention to the fact that the shrubbery is, indeed, dead.

A sickly woman with filthy hair bolting from her head, tubes up her nose, and IV lines running everywhere is not improved by blue eyeshadow and red lipstick. But if you wish to look like Bette Davis in *What Ever Happened to Baby Jane?*, go ahead.

Save the makeup for your release. Everyone who's seen you looking like chicken gravy will be stunned by the contrast and say brilliant things like "Well, you're certainly looking better!" The doctor will, of course, credit his own remarkable healing skills for your startling beauty.

# 9
# DOLLARS AND CENTS

## FOR LITTLE MORE THAN IT WOULD COST TO OUTFIT COMMUNIST CHINA IN PENDLETON BLAZERS, YOU TOO CAN HAVE SURGERY

*The markup on everyday items used by patients in a hospital makes government-contract screwdrivers and toilet seats look like a Blue Light Special.*

The thing to remember about the high cost of medical care is that none of the stuff you are being billed for actually costs that much. . . . They just charge you that much. The unsuspecting patient, however, most often is unaware that he is being charged for AB-SOLUTELY EVERYTHING. Unlike your major hotel chains, nothing comes with the room.

The nurses are expertly trained salespeople, working on commission, who do not have to tell you that they are *selling* you whatever it is they are offering. ("Would you like a pillow?" "Would you like some toilet paper?")

These items actually have computer bar codes on them, which the nurse removes and collects for the accounting person who comes to your room each day to tally your purchases.

If you try to circumvent this, settling in with your own toothpaste and hand lotion, you will be informed that these items are lethal prescription drugs regulated by the FDA.

## DRUMMING UP BUSINESS: YOUR PHYSICIAN'S MARKETING STRATEGY

Medicine is big business requiring a steady stream of new and repeat customers. Since it would be tacky to solicit names of sick friends, doctors will try to uncover something else that is wrong with you. This is taught in a course entitled *Diagnosis and Financial Planning.*

In the absence of anything *actually* wrong with you, doctors will suggest removal of and/or treatment of some body part that *may* cause you problems in the future because it *probably, may perhaps, could possibly* flare up, oh, twenty, thirty years down the road. Or at least it does in alcoholic Peruvian asbestos workers who bathe in raw sewage.

So, why not just take care of it now?

If you don't buy this, they take it as a personal affront. They get whiny and irritable, and they'll sulk and pout. ("But I *wanna* take out your gallbladder!")

## YOUR BILL OF (THIS CAN'T BE) RIGHTS

You are entitled, by law, to an accounting of all charges.

However, the staggering sum you are spending does not entitle you to an *accurate* accounting, particularly if you're insured. This would force cutbacks on expensive, unnecessary tests and limit charges to Services Actually Performed.

Uninsured patients are charged only for Care Actually Received, since they can't pay anyway. Consequently, you must be charged for Care You Didn't Receive to make up for that shortfall. This helps the economy, so when you are penniless and the insurance companies go broke, Medicaid can pick up the slack.

So you see why you must be sent bills that look like this:

| | | | |
|---|---|---|---|
| Supplies | $10,786.23 | Other Supplies | $11,447.00 |
| Pharmacy | $18,003.21 | Facilities | $42,780.00 |
| Tests | $59,467.88 | Other Tests | $22,554.66 |
| Facilities | $42,780.00 | Room & Board | $33,565.75 |
| Medical Stuff | $47,005.99 | Party Favors | $ 1,750.00 |

## ACCOUNTS RECEIVABLE

The helpful personnel in Accounts Receivable are trained to emit loud, indignant bursts of air into the telephone and put you on hold if you call and request an itemized bill.

They will come on the line several hours later and ask you your address, despite the fact they are staring right at it, along with your entire personal medical history, credit history, wedding gift registry, shoe size, and Average Daily Urine Output. ("Hey, Gwen. Line two's a gusher.")

It will take them several months to make up an itemized list that exactly matches the total of the statement they sent you. ("Hey, Gwen. I gotta come up with $3,201.04 more for 'Miscellaneous Other.' What should I put down?")

Of course, during this time you will be sent increasingly vicious demands for payment. When you finally receive the itemization, it will be in cuneiform.

## BILL TERMINOLOGY

You will learn, to your surprise, that you were charged $51 for a 2" × 3" colclasure phreboxis pad. Tireless investigation will reveal that this was a piece of paper you had requested to dispose of the night nurse's gum.

You'll find that you were charged $89 for the felt-tipped marker used to print the sign "DO NOT GIVE THIS PATIENT ANY FOOD OR WATER." The service fee for skipping a meal was $165.

You'll also get a separate bill from anyone who ever even remotely touched your case. In addition to the people you remember, you will receive a bill from:

- A doctor you never heard of who happened to glance at you by mistake while you were lying in the corridor (Observation, $100)
- A woman who mistakenly picked up your pictures at the Photomat (Radiology, $225)
- A physical therapist who nudged you in the elevator (Manipulation, $185)
- A doctor who stuttered when asked about your condition (Consultation, $150; second opinion, $225)

## INSURANCE

Sorting out your bills is, of course, impossible. The insurance statements will have no apparent correlation to anything for which the hospital is billing you.

Your first insurance statement will list everything as a non-covered expense or co-payment item and advise you that you have not met your deductible. If you call and complain, you'll get a second statement—something that looks like this:

| Patient | Prov | Serv | Totl | ElChgs | Less n/pd | Amt | Explntn |
|---------|------|------|------|--------|-----------|-----|---------|
| M. Smith | ComHos | *&^ ^ | $745 | $140 | $100 | $705 | R.2#/@>7^ |

Code

| | |
|---|---|
| R.2 | This is not a covered expense. |
| # | The amount exceeds negotiated limits. |
| / | Provider is not an approved vendor. |
| @ | Procedure is ridiculous. |
| > | You could have done this at home. |
| 7 | No such treatment exists. |
| ^ | Outlawed after the Inquisition. |
| * | Policy does not extend to veterinary services. |
| & | Give us a minute, we'll come up with something. |

You will receive approximately 5,400 of these things in the mail, all in separate envelopes, over a period of six years.

All calls to the insurance carrier are transferred to the nation's busiest airline, where you will be informed by a recording that your call is important to them and will be answered in the order in which it was received. While you're holding, you can do some little chore, like growing tomatoes from seed.

## PROCEDURE FOR HANDLING BILLS AND INSURANCE STATEMENTS

- All bills and statements should be placed, unopened, into a shoe box and stored under the bed.
- When the first shoe box is filled, buy another pair of shoes.
- In four or five months, retrieve the boxes and dump them on the floor. Open all the bills, putting the bills in one pile and the envelopes in another. Discard the envelopes and return the bills to the box. You now have room to store bills for five more months.
- In about a year, when the doctor has said it's OK to have a drink or two, pour yourself a stiff one and drag out the boxes.
- Call each provider and request an itemized accounting of all transactions, since you've been trying for a year now to figure out their screwy accounting system.
- Take only the bills with death threats stamped in red ink and note the balance. Write a check for that amount, moving the decimal point over two places to the left.
- Go out and buy another pair of shoes. (This might be tax-deductible as "Office Supplies.")

## YOUR FILE AND RECORDS AS MEMORABILIA

Using your itemized statement, put together a scrapbook to chronicle your stay. Repressed experiences will resurface as you note each entry. Also, demand your complete file on all procedures, tests, and lab results.

The hospital won't want to release this, of course. They'll act as if you plan to duplicate the procedures at home with unsterilized vegetable peelers. Actually, they're afraid you'll use this information in court.

Be persistent. Park yourself in the medical records office with a barking, productive cough. Expectorate into tissues and throw them on the floor. Eventually, they'll give in.

Once you have your records, you can relive each precious moment whenever you're feeling sentimental. Sit back with a cup of General Foods International Coffee and savor the heartwarming details of that excruciating spinal tap. Chuckle at the coy reference to your aboriginal screeching as mild discomfort.

Put all of this into a leather-bound album along with cards from well-wishers and tastefully matted prints of X-rays and ultrasound photos. Set it on your coffee table for interested guests.

They'll be amazed that you survived it all—and even more amazed that you could afford to pay for it. Best of all, they won't stay long, so you can curl up in front of the TV and finally get to see an entire segment of "Geraldo."

# APPENDIX

## AN APPARENTLY FUNCTIONLESS PART
## THAT SHOULD BE REMOVED

*No medical manual would be
complete without an appendix.
Like all appendixes, however,
this appendix is not necessary
to the survival of the manual
and should probably be
removed.*

## HOSPITAL SURVIVAL STRATEGIES

- Amuse yourself with the bar codes on hospital supplies. With a number 2 pencil (of the sort you'd use for multiple-choice preemployment screening tests asking you if you are now, or have been in the past, a serial killer), fill in a few white spaces. You may wind up paying $142 for that Kleenex, but the week's worth of antibiotics for $1.39 will make it worthwhile.
- A camcorder with audio, set on a tripod and equipped with remote, is a dandy little privacy-getter.
- Whenever you're given medication or subjected to a procedure, make methodical notes in a journal or dictate quietly into a mini cassette recorder. (It is unimportant if you actually take notes. Whisper the words to "Louie, Louie" if you like. The mere impression of record keeping is sufficient.)
- Open the telephone book to "Attorneys" and put it next to the phone.
- Offhandedly mention the book you intend to write about this.
- Claim that you are allergic to most foods and that the only things you can tolerate are Domino's pizza, Godiva chocolates, Haagen Dazs ice cream, and fresh oranges from Harry and David's.
- Send yourself flowers from the current U.S. President. (Or, if you're in a hospital with a name like Our Lady of Perpetual Misery,

from the Pope.) You'll be amazed how your care improves.

• Your doctors aren't coming in often enough? Refuse a test or procedure. They'll be all over you in seconds.

• Have a friend bring in a copy of *Medical Malpractice: A National Disgrace.* Lay it open across your chest just before drifting off to sleep.

• To determine the necessity of a procedure, advise the staff that insurance will not cover this test.

• Before each procedure represented as painless, advise the technician that if it does hurt, you WILL set fire to his hair.

• A talented photography editor can produce a convincing group picture of you with Phil Donahue, Geraldo, Oprah, Joan Rivers, and Maury Povich to place at your bedside. Follow it up with a balloon bouquet and a card reading, "Can't wait to have you on the show. Kisses."

• If you want a private room at no extra charge, sing to your roommate. "A Hundred Bottles of Beer on the Wall" is good. So is "Don't Worry, Be Happy." Call out his name continually from 4:00 A.M. to 6:00 A.M. Tell him you once disemboweled a llama.

• Find out who dispenses the pain medication. Continually praise and flatter her. Liberally use words such as "blessed," "sainted," and "extraordinarily beautiful."

- When your primary dealer is off duty, moan wrenchingly, like a wounded rhino, until the person in the next bed threatens to murder you with his fork. To avoid this unpleasantness, they'll simply administer the mass quantities of morphine you deserve.
- Secretly tell each nurse she's the best, the only one you can trust to get things right.
- If praise is ineffective, announce your intention to rename your dog. You will enjoy waking it up at 3:00 A.M. and saying, "Roll over, Nurse!"

Stay well, my friend.